NORTH SEA

Hull●

●STERFIELD

Grimsby

●STURTON le STEEPLE

THE WASH

Boston●

ENGLAND

●Cambridge

RIVER THAMES

AMSTERDAM

●Leyden

●Delfshaven

THE LOW COUNTRIES

●LONDON

●Dover

●Calais

ENGLISH CHANNEL

FRANCE

A NEW LOOK
AT THE
PILGRIMS
Why They Came to America

A NEW LOOK AT THE PILGRIMS

Why They Came to America

by Beatrice Siegel

Illustrated by
Douglas Morris

Walker And Company
New York

First published in the United States of America in 1977 by the Walker Publishing Company, Inc.

Published simultaneously in Canada by Fitzhenry & Whiteside, Limited, Toronto.

Trade ISBN: 0-8027-6291-3
Reinforced ISBN: 0-8027-6292-1

Library of Congress Catalog Card Number: 76-57060

Printed in the United States of America.

10 9 8 7 6 5 4 3 2 1

TO ANDRA AND JULIA

Contents

A NEW LOOK
AT THE
PILGRIMS
Why They Came to America

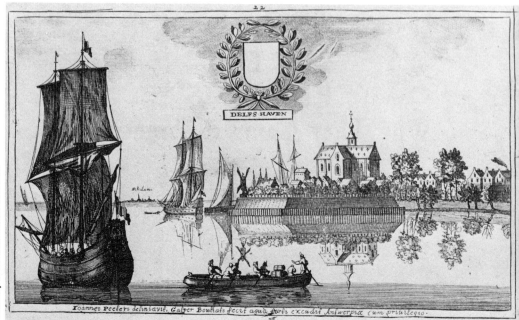

DELFS HAVEN

Ioannes Peeters deliniavit. Gaſper Bouttats fecit aqua forti excudit Antwerpiæ cum priuilegio.

Introduction

EVERYBODY KNOWS THAT the Pilgrims sailed to America on the *Mayflower* and settled in Plymouth, Massachusetts.

From the stories we have heard they were brave, God-fearing, hard-working people. We worship them as heroes and think of them as people who had no faults. But they were human beings like you and me with good qualities and bad ones.

We are going to poke around in history a bit to find out what they were like *before* they made that brave voyage across the Atlantic Ocean. What kind of people were they? Did they come to the New World only to seek religious freedom, or were there other reasons?

In questions and answers we hope to take a new look at the Pilgrims, to tell who they were, how they lived in their native land, and the many different reasons they came to settle in this country.

Where Did the Pilgrims Come From?

To get to the beginning of the Pilgrim story we must turn time back hundreds of years to the 1600s. And we must go back across the Atlantic Ocean to England, for that is where the Pilgrims were born and grew up.

A few lived in the city of London. Many came from the nearby towns. But the leaders of the Pilgrims, those who made the decision to leave the land of their birth, grew up in the north of England in the region of Scrooby. Sometimes it is called Pilgrim land.

Scrooby was a poor village. Hundreds of years ago it was described as a "meane Townlet." In its center stood the parish church, St. Wilfred's, and a few cottages. Other cottages were tucked away in the rolling hills of the countryside. Yet this poor village boasted

ST. WILFRED'S CHURCH, SCROOBY

a large manor house within a moat with its own bakery, brewery, barns and stables, granaries, kennels, and a chapel.

The village stood on the main highway between London and Edinburgh, Scotland. Though it was called the Great North Road, it was only a narrow dirt lane traveled by horses, for coaches were not yet in use. Members of the aristocracy who used this road were put up at the manor house. They enjoyed hunting the red deer in the surrounding fields. Or they hunted the plentiful game in nearby Sherwood Forest, where Robin Hood was said to have lived.

How did they earn a living?

Most of them were poor, uneducated people burdened with hard lives.

In the Scrooby region they worked on the land. A few rented small plots from the manor house and became tenant farmers. Others worked for a regular wage as farm laborers. The men tilled the land and planted and harvested crops, but despite their hard work they could barely make ends meet.

Women also worked from morning to night tending the house and helping in the fields. In winter they sat at their looms weaving a rough cloth they later cut and sewed into clothes.

Those who lived in London and the nearby towns worked as apprentices, artisans, or petty tradespeople. Their homes were in the poor sections of the cities.

There were a few exceptions.

William Bradford, growing up near Scrooby in the village of Austerfield, came from a farming family. By the time he was nine years old, both his parents had died. He was brought up by aunts and uncles, who expected him to become a farmer.

William Brewster grew up on the estate of the manor house, where his father was bailiff, or manager. Young William was sent to Cambridge University for an education. He found students and teachers vigorously debating new ideas. And although he was only a boy of fifteen, he never forgot the discussions he heard about religion and the new ways of worshiping God.

What was England like in those days?

It was "merrie England" for the rich. They led fairy tale lives of luxury. In palatial homes they wore their extravagant clothes made of velvet and lace, of jewel-encrusted brocade and taffeta. They dined at tables that groaned under mountains of food.

For amusement there were masquerades, hunts, and the theater of Shakespeare. Poets sang carefree songs. The poet Christopher Marlowe wrote:

Come live with me, and be my love,
And we will all the pleasures prove . . .

Daredevil buccaneers like Francis Drake and Walter Raleigh explored distant seas in small wooden vessels. They brought back a rich booty of treasure from ships and countries they plundered on the way.

And there was a new class of people—merchants growing rich on trade and commerce.

But "merrie England" did not exist for the poor, who were the majority of the people. For pleasure they met together in the church or the alehouse. On Sundays they practiced archery, played ball, or hunted small game. Occasionally they enjoyed themselves at a village fair. But by and large they lived in a

SIR WALTER RALEIGH　　　　**SIR FRANCIS DRAKE**

dingy, mean world. Many were always hungry, barely nourished on a diet of porridge, bread, and a rare scrap of fish or meat.

Thousands could find no work and were forced into a life of crime. When caught, they were cruelly punished. Men and women were publicly whipped on bare backs for very minor offenses. Or they were put on public display in a pillory, a wooden frame in which their hands and head were locked. Just for stealing a loaf of bread a person could be sentenced to be hanged.

Some became beggars rather than criminals. They swarmed over the streets of London. Or they walked from village to village pleading for handouts from

THE PILLORY

churches and homes. But poverty made people mean and unfriendly. Many drove the beggars from their towns rather than share their own meager food with them. A nursery rhyme of the time tells about this.

> Hark! Hark! the dogs bark,
>   The beggars are coming to town;
> Some in rags and some in tags,
>   And some in silken gowns.

> Some gave them white bread,
>   And some gave them brown,
> And some gave them a good horse-whip,
>   And sent them out of town.

What was religion like in England at that time?

In those days everyone had to belong to the Church of England and worship according to its regulations. No other form of worship was permitted. At the head of the Church of England was the queen or king, for government and religion were tied together and ruled by the same person.

If people talked out against the church, it meant they were also talking against the government, and this was a serious crime.

Queen Elizabeth I, and after her King James I, called people who opposed the Church of England *Nonconformists*. There were laws against them. They could be arrested and thrown into jail, sometimes for life. Nonconformist leaders were hung at the gallows.

King James justified his rule of the church as well as the government when he announced that God had given him the right to rule. He called it ruling by "divine right" and said, "Kings are God's lieutenants and sit on God's throne. . . ."

QUEEN ELIZABETH I
(Reigned 1558–1603)

KING JAMES I
(Reigned 1603–1625)

Why Did the Pilgrims Disobey the Rulers of England?

THE PILGRIMS DID NOT MEAN to disobey their rulers. They considered themselves loyal subjects of Queen Elizabeth and King James. But they despised the Church of England, and they refused to worship there. It was corrupt, they said, with pompous rituals and ceremonies and rich bishops in fancy embroidered robes. Although these bishops knew nothing about the local problems, they appointed the minister for every village. It was the minister who told people what to think and what was in the Bible.

But the Bible had been translated into English, and some people could read it for themselves. What they read was different from what their minister told them. They could find nothing that justified the fancy ceremonies of the establishment church.

At first they tried to change the church from within. Then they said it was hopeless. They took a radical step and seceded completely from the church.

They called themselves Separatists because henceforth they would be separated from the sinful government and its sinful Church of England.

In this way they were different from the Puritans who remained within the Church of England and tried to reform it.

What did the Separatists believe?

They believed the church must be pure and simple. And its members must be pure in thought and action. Because they modeled themselves after the saints of the Scriptures, the Separatists are often called the Saints.

In their church there would be no bishops. There would be no ornaments like altars, candles, and incense. And there would be no set prayer book. Instrumental music would be forbidden, for to them the organ was the "divil's bagpipes."

Each church would be independent, complete in itself. For wherever people gathered, they could set up their own church or congregation. In their "Congregation of Saints," all would be equal in the eyes of God.

Merriment on Sundays? Sinful, said the Separatists. It was God's day, and they turned it into a full day of sermons and prayers.

Plain folk were attracted to the gospel of the Separatists. It gave them a new feeling, as if chains had been struck from their bodies and souls. They could choose their own minister. They could talk up, discuss the meaning of the Bible, and help make decisions. Always before this the government and the appointed minister had told them what to do, what to think.

What did the Separatists do about it?

Despite government threats of arrest secret churches were formed in many parts of England.

In 1606 the Separatists in the Scrooby region took the dangerous step of setting up their own secret church. William Brewster arranged for them to meet each week in a room of the manor house.

THE MANOR HOUSE, SCROOBY

William Bradford, then a young man of seventeen, attended these secret meetings. Every week he walked the two miles from his home in Austerfield to Scrooby. But his uncles opposed his radical activity. To avoid constant arguments with them he moved in with the Brewster family, where he was treated like a son.

The preacher John Robinson and his wife, Bridget, also came to the secret church meetings from nearby Sturton le Steeple. John Robinson later became the leading teacher of the Scrooby sect.

It was the group of Separatists meeting in Scrooby who would become the leaders of the Pilgrim movement.

[15]

Why were the rulers of England afraid of them?

The Separatists, and other Nonconformists, spoke dangerous words.

They used words like *freedom, equality, individual, liberty of conscience.*

The rulers of England felt threatened. If common people claimed they were equal before God, they might then claim they should be equal in the eyes of government. They might tell the king how they should be ruled and even question his rights. Freedom of worship might let loose a flood of other demands like freedom of speech and freedom of thought. Where would it end?

The government decided it was dangerous to let common people regulate their own lives in such a way. It forbade all private religious meetings. And King James, angry at the dissenters, demanded that everyone had to belong to the Church of England and conform to its rules. He threatened those who did not conform with jail or death.

Why Did the Separatists Decide to Leave England?

THE GOVERNMENT UNLEASHED a reign of terror against Nonconformists. Agents hunted them down, arrested them, and threw them into dungeons.

Terror struck the Scrooby Separatists when word leaked out about their secret meetings. William Brewster was summoned to appear before the court to account for his religious dissension. Luckily he was only fined.

But the Scrooby sect knew danger was close. In addition to police terror, friends and neighbors turned against them. They began to pry into their lives and act as informers. Villagers jeered at the Separatists and made fun of their cold, "uppity" ways. They found the Separatists aloof, filled with self-importance as if they were really God's chosen people.

THE SEPARATISTS IN PRISON

Separatist children became frightened at the name-calling. And they were lonely because their friends were not permitted to visit them.

Fearful for their lives and miserable because of the persecution by their neighbors, the Scrooby group decided to leave England. It was a painful decision to leave the land they loved, to tear up their ties to generations of ancestors.

To get together money for their escape they quietly began to sell off their few furnishings and possessions.

Why did they choose Holland?

Religious dissenters knew that Holland was liberal in granting freedom of worship. It had become a haven for people persecuted in England and France.

Many English dissenters had already fled there and had established a Separatist church in Amsterdam. The Scrooby group decided to seek safety with their brethren in this small country across the North Sea.

Why did they leave England in secret?

It was not easy to leave England.

The law stated that anyone leaving the country had to get permission from the government. The Separatists knew that the government regarded them as traitors and would never grant them the necessary papers.

Day after day the children found the grownups clustered together in secret conversations. At dusk they scurried with their parents across empty fields to different meeting places. They heard arguments among the grownups and then "hush, hush" as their voices sank again to whispers.

The frightened Separatists finally discovered a way to get out of England. They bribed the captain of an English ship with a large fee, and he agreed to sail them to Holland.

How Did They Escape from England?

THE SEPARATISTS OF SCROOBY planned their escape for the end of 1607. One dark night men, women, and children started their long, dangerous journey. They stole quietly across country to the seaport of Boston on England's east coast. They waited for the captain near a small creek. Two nights later he showed up and led them aboard his ship. He collected his fee—and then he betrayed them to the police.

The police boarded the ship. They loaded the Separatists into small boats and rowed them back to shore. Sailors robbed them of their money, books, and other precious possessions.

The police marched the Separatists through Boston. Townspeople lined the streets and jeered at the poor frightened families trying to flee from England. They were locked up in cells in the Guildhall for a month. A few were kept longer, but finally all were freed and ordered back to their hometowns.

THE ARREST IN BOSTON, ENGLAND

They planned another escape for the spring of 1608. This time a Dutch skipper agreed to sail them to Holland. They arranged to meet on a deserted stretch of marshland between the hamlets of Hull and Grimsby.

Women, children, and belongings were loaded onto a bark on the River Ryton. It sailed down the winding rivers to the secret meeting place. There the boat got stuck in the mud at low tide.

In the meantime Bradford, Brewster, Robinson, and the older boys along with the other men walked forty miles to the meeting place. They found the women and children shivering with cold in the boat grounded in the muddy flats. They had to wait for a rising tide to float the boat.

The next morning the Dutch skipper anchored his ship nearby. He sent over a dinghy to bring some of the men aboard. Bradford and a few others had just boarded the vessel when they saw a mob of villagers on foot and on horse, armed with guns and clubs, coming toward the women and children. The men still on shore ran to help the terrified families.

When the Dutch skipper saw the mob, he was afraid he would be arrested and thrown into jail. He quickly pulled up anchor and sailed away.

The Dutch ship headed for Holland across the North Sea. Suddenly a terrible storm broke out. Wild winds and mountainous waves battered the vessel. Black storm clouds hid the sun by day and the moon and stars at night, so navigation was difficult. The ship was forced off course toward the coast of Norway. The sailors cried out, "We sink! We sink!" But Bradford and the other Separatists on board began to pray. It seemed a miracle when the storm subsided and the seamen could steer the ship back on course again.

The ship finally reached Amsterdam. The voyage had taken fourteen days instead of the usual two to make the crossing from England.

The weeping, frightened women and children left behind in the boat stuck on the muddy flats were arrested. Police hauled them from one place to another, from one justice to another. The authorities did not know what to do with them. They could not be returned to their villages, for their homes had been sold. And they were innocent of any crime. Finally the officials decided to let them go on their way. The Separatist men who had stayed to help them arranged for their departure for Holland. In one way or another all the Scrooby Separatists reached Amsterdam by the summer of 1608.

But life in Amsterdam was not peaceful. Serious religious quarrels broke out among the members of the congregation creating splits and factions. After a year the Scrooby group decided to move to another city, where, by themselves, they could follow their own religious beliefs. They chose Leyden, forty miles away.

What Kind of City Was Leyden?

LEYDEN WAS A BEAUTIFUL old city. It had broad cobblestone streets and gabled stone houses. Quiet canals wound through the town. And windmills towered high above the flat countryside.

The city hummed with handicrafts and industries. It was the center for a bustling textile trade. Families worked long hours at looms in their homes weaving fabric. Others worked in factories and fields washing, drying, and stretching the cloth.

But the University of Leyden, a center for free discussion, was its greatest attraction. Students and teachers gathered there from all parts of Europe. The halls of colleges and the streets of the town rang with heated arguments. Students debated new ideas in religion, politics, and art. A wonderful sense of freedom filled them with energy and excitement. It was as if they were awaking to a new life.

A LEYDEN FAMILY

Where did they settle in Leyden?

After a couple of years in Leyden, in 1611, the Separatists scraped together enough money to buy a large old house. It stood on Bell Alley in a neighborhood of narrow, damp lanes and tangled streets. Close by were the University of Leyden and the huge stone structure of St. Peter's Church, formerly a Roman Catholic cathedral.

They named the house Green Gate. The large main floor became a meeting hall. There they gathered for prayers and for social and business meetings. The upstairs was turned into an apartment for Pastor Robinson, his wife, Bridget, and their three children, John, Bridget, and Isaac.

Small attached cottages were built in back of the house around a garden. Here poor members of the sect lived. Other Separatists found quarters near one another on the narrow streets. The Brewster family lived on Stink Alley. William Bradford settled into his own home with his sixteen-year-old wife, Dorothy May, whom he had met in Amsterdam.

A few newcomers became active in the Green Gate congregation. There was Robert Cushman, a wool comber by trade. He lived with his wife and son, Thomas, on Nuns Alley. John Carver, brother-in-law of Pastor Robinson, owned his own home. He was a wealthy merchant and a deacon of the Separatist Church.

What kind of work did they do?

In England they had been farmers. In Holland they had to start all over again, learn new trades, and adjust to life in a city. They became weavers, tailors, carpenters, barbers. One made hats, another gloves. One cobbled shoes, another dyed cloth.

William Bradford became a corduroy maker. William Brewster taught English to Dutch students. His sixteen-year-old son, Jonathan, became a ribbon maker.

They worked from early morning to late at night every day but the Sabbath. And even though they worked hard, many lived at starvation level.

Did the children work?

Children had to work to help support the family. They found jobs in the trades and like their parents worked long hours. Because they were children, they earned very low wages. But that little extra money often meant food on the table.

It upset the parents to see their children grow pale, tired, and sickly from the hard work. They no longer looked like children. They seemed old long before their time.

Children of poor families usually worked in those days. And they were always sickly. The Separatist children had helped on farms back home in Scrooby, England. But in Leyden they worked indoors in the cloth industry. The bad conditions and long hours damaged their health. They began to look like other poor city children.

Did they speak Dutch?

The adult Separatists never learned to speak the Dutch language. It was too "guttural," they said.

But the young children learned to speak the language while playing with their little Dutch friends.

Were they lonely for England?

They were so homesick they would have returned at once to England if the king had promised not to persecute them. They wanted to be surrounded by familiar faces, hear their native tongue, and walk on beloved stretches of land.

Though the Dutch were kind, the Separatists lived like exiles among them. They formed an English community and held on to their old way of life. English was the only language they spoke, and they insisted their children speak English, too. As far as they were concerned, they were still subjects of the king of England.

Why Did They Decide to Leave Leyden?

DURING THEIR MANY YEARS in Leyden the Separatists had to face painful facts. They met often during the years 1617, 1618, and 1619 to discuss their problems. It was true they could worship freely in Holland, but it was not enough.

The group of worshipers in the Green Gate Church was getting smaller instead of increasing. When old members died, no one replaced them. The Separatists in England preferred to face persecution at home rather than the hardships in Leyden.

They were also worried about their children, who were attracted to the Dutch way of life. It was a joyful one, with dancing, laughter, and merry celebrations on Sundays. How could they save their children for the godly life when they were surrounded by what they considered sin and corruption?

DUTCH CHILDREN

How did the children feel?

The children resented the strict discipline and rigid beliefs of their parents. And they resented their parents' efforts to bring them up as if they were English. They were growing up in Holland, and they felt more Dutch than English.

They did not want to attend the strict Separatist Church. On Sundays young children sat in a separate section under the watchful eye of the deaconess. She boxed children's ears if they talked or laughed. Or worse, she whipped them with a birch rod. From outdoors came the happy sounds of Dutch children playing and having fun. That is where they wanted to be —outdoors. Instead they were cooped up for the whole day, forced to listen to endless sermons and hymns.

Many older children decided their own futures. They married into Dutch families. Boys signed up on Dutch ships and sailed to foreign ports.

What happened to William Brewster?

Something mysterious was going on. And it had to do with their favorite elder, William Brewster.

Brewster had become a printer and the owner of a printing press, which was installed in the attic of his home. With the help of a master printer and a young Separatist apprentice, Edward Winslow, he turned out religious books. But, more important, he secretly turned out pamphlets attacking the king of England and the Church of England.

These illegal pamphlets were smuggled into Scotland and England in vats to look like a shipment of French wine.

Officials there discovered the illegal pamphlets and quickly reported it to the government. King James became enraged. "Arrest those guilty of this seditious act," he roared.

England demanded that the Dutch government turn the traitors over to them. Dutch police searched the country for Brewster, identified as the leader. But he had vanished, gone underground. No one knew whether he was in Holland or England.

To add to all these worries, there was talk of war between Protestant Holland and Catholic Spain. War meant death, pestilence, famine. And if Catholic Spain won, it would end freedom of worship for the Separatists.

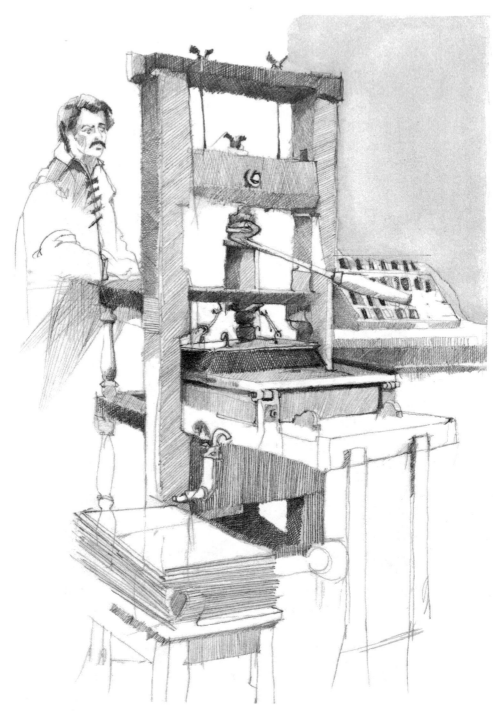

PRINTING PRESS

The Separatists of the Green Gate congregation felt beset on all sides. They decided they had to find a new sanctuary even if it meant another terrible uprooting.

It was not dissent driving them from Holland but discontent over other matters. They looked for a country where they could worship freely, where their church would be safe from sin and corruption, and where they could have a better economic life.

Why Did They Choose America?

AMERICA—A WONDERFUL NEW WORLD across the Atlantic Ocean—excited people's imaginations. Explorers, seamen, and fishermen returned from there with glowing stories. They told about a vast "empty" land of dense forests filled with fruit and nut trees where seeds quickly sprouted in the fertile soil. Fish were so plentiful along the coast they were easily caught in nets. And there was a new profitable trade in furs.

England had already established a colony in Jamestown, Virginia. A former governor of Jamestown, the explorer Captain John Smith, had sailed his ship along the New England coast to map its harbors.

Smith wrote a book, *A Description of New England*, that was so popular it was passed from hand to hand. In his book Smith advertised the wonders of the New World and urged people to settle there.

CAPTAIN JOHN SMITH

There were long, heated discussions among the Leyden Separatists about where next to go. Should it be North America, or should they try Guiana on the coast of South America? Walter Raleigh and other explorers had described Guiana as a rich paradise where tropical weather made life easy. But the majority of the congregation preferred a colony near their countrymen in Virginia.

America seemed ready-made for them. It was a land unstained by sin. They would be able to support themselves. They could bring up their children to be true believers. And in its deep forests, far from the corrupt world of Europe, they could build their community to God.

Were they afraid to go to America?

At first the entire Green Gate congregation of about one hundred people agreed to migrate to America. But as time went on many changed their minds.

The ill and the elderly were filled with terror at the idea of crossing the dangerous Atlantic Ocean. They knew that countrymen of theirs, 130 of them, had earlier died at sea while making the crossing in a small ship. They had perished from lack of water, hunger, and sickness.

Others had great fears of the unknown, of the wilderness of the New World. They had visions that they would die of starvation. Or that they would have to go naked for lack of clothing. They saw themselves suffering from the change of air, the different food, the new drinking water.

Many were afraid they would meet a savage death at the hands of the Indians. Terrible stories circulated among them about the Indians being cruel, dangerous, and merciless when angry.

By the time the project was ready to get going, only forty young, bold members of the congregation were determined to see the voyage through. They felt confident they could overcome all obstacles.

Among those who decided to go were William Brewster, William Bradford, John Carver, Robert Cushman, Edward Winslow, and Isaac Allerton. These men and their families would form the backbone of the Pilgrim movement.

Who had to given them permission to settle there?

England had staked out her claim to vast stretches of territory in North America. Other European countries had also carved out parcels of land. The rulers of Europe saw in the New World an opportunity to extend their power and increase their wealth. They justified taking over this land by calling the Indians of America a heathen and savage people. As Christian nations they felt free to do this.

Christianity was the only true religion, they said. And it was their duty and their right to occupy the land of non-Christians in order to introduce the benefits of the Christian faith.

The band of Leyden Separatists, seeking a shelter in the New World, had to turn to King James I of England for permission to settle there.

How did they get permission?

The Separatists knew the King of England despised them as radicals and troublemakers. Yet they needed his approval to settle in America. They also wanted the right to worship there freely.

To work this out, they sent two trusted members of the group to England. They were Robert Cushman and John Carver.

These men took with them a statement of the Separatists' beliefs called *Seven Articles*. In it the Separatists played down their differences with the Church of England.

Neither the king of England nor his bishops was fooled. But England was expanding. She needed strong, determined people to be pioneers in an unknown world. It would make it easier for the government to hold on to its territorial claims if people actually settled on the land.

The King did not approve the project with the official stamp of the Great Seal. But he did say he would not hinder the Separatists nor "molest them provided they carried themselves peaceably." This

THE SEPARATISTS
APPEAL TO KING JAMES

partial approval discouraged many members of the congregation. Nevertheless, it helped them get a grant of land for a settlement in the New World.

Did They Have Money for the Voyage?

THE SEPARATISTS OF the Green Gate congregation pooled together their savings and money from the sale of belongings. They collected contributions from friends. One or two wealthy people helped out. But they could not raise enough money for a safe voyage.

They needed large sums to buy a ship, repair it, provision it with food and other necessities, and hire a crew. They had to buy enough supplies for the voyage as well as for the first few months in the New World.

It became a critical situation. Unless they raised the funds, their dream of sailing to America would be ended.

Who offered to help them?

The first offer of help came from Dutch businessmen. The Dutch had a trading post at the mouth of the Hudson River called New Amsterdam (now New York City). They offered generous support if the Separatists would settle there. The Dutch needed colonizers to strengthen their position, especially against the English, their competitors for the land.

The Separatists were not happy about these negotiations. It meant they would have to become Dutch citizens. They had hoped to settle under the English flag.

Who were the merchant adventurers?

In the midst of their discussions with the Dutch, the Separatists were visited by an Englishman, Thomas Weston. He was an ironmonger by trade. But he was also an aggressive businessman. He offered to raise money in England for the Separatists. They happily accepted his offer of support.

Businessmen, or capitalists, in England at that time were often called merchant adventurers. They made up a growing class of people who were getting rich in industry and trade. They invested their money in new business ventures in order to make a profit.

Weston pulled together seventy merchant adventurers who agreed to back the Separatists' project. They did not share the religious views of the Separatists. It was the idea of a quick profit from a colony in America that interested them.

The Separatists and merchant adventurers formed a partnership and wrote up a seven-year contract. It was a long agreement. In general, the businessmen agreed to supply a ship, load it with provisions, and take care of the emigrants during the time it took them to build their colony.

The Separatists agreed to work hard and to ship from the New World back to England merchandise that the businessmen could sell for a profit. They would send fur, fish, lumber, sassafras, and whatever else they could get by trading with the Indians. At the end of seven years all would share in the profits of the company.

Did others join the voyage?

The merchant adventurers were upset to learn that only some forty Separatists—more than half of them children—would be making the voyage. Such a small band could hardly build a safe, profitable colony in the wilderness of America! To ensure success the businessmen signed on additional volunteers. The new recruits from London and southwestern England accepted the terms of the agreement and promised to work hard to make the colony a success.

These new recruits became known as the Strangers. They were strangers to each other as well as to the Saints. Unlike the Saints they were not motivated to uproot their lives for religious reasons. Most of them belonged to the Church of England simply because they were brought up in that faith.

What they had in common with the Separatists was their economic class. They were poor, dispossessed, with no voice in the government. They joined the project to find a better life in the New World.

Why Did They Need Two Ships?

ARRANGEMENTS WERE MADE for the voyage to America to take place in the summer of 1620.

In the spring of that year the Leyden Separatists carried out their plan to buy a ship. The foundation of their project was to own one. They would sail in it to America, where the ship and crew would stay with them for one year. They would use the vessel for fishing, for trading up and down the coast, and for whatever other purposes they thought necessary.

They found a small cargo vessel in the shipyards of Holland. She was called the *Speedwell.* Her skipper was a man named Reynolds.

The merchant adventurers, on the other hand, planned to rent a ship. It would be large enough to hold the London emigrants and the bulk of provisions. The ship would remain in America only until the colonists could load it with merchandise. She

THE SPEEDWELL

would then return to England, where the businessmen would sell off the cargo for a profit.

Toward the summer of 1620 the merchant adventurers chartered a ship. She was called the *Mayflower*. Her skipper was Christopher Jones.

The *Speedwell* with the Leyden Separatists would meet the *Mayflower* with the London emigrants in Southampton, England. They would be companion ships during the ocean crossing. Each would provide protection for the other against piracy at sea and in

THE MAYFLOWER

the event of emergencies. Night and day, on a stormy ocean or a calm one, they would keep each other in sight.

What kind of ships were the Speedwell and the Mayflower?

Very little is known about the *Speedwell* and the *Mayflower* except that they were cargo ships. They had carried merchandise coastwise and across the seas to foreign ports.

There were no passenger ships in those days. The cargo ships available were filthy, infested with disease-carrying bugs and rats. They smelled foul from their cargo, especially if it was fish.

A cabin for the captain might be found on a large ship like the *Mayflower*. But there were no other beds and no bathrooms—only buckets for toilet purposes.

The crew slept wherever they could—on bare decks or on a spare blanket or on a coil of rope. Sometimes they slept in hammocks. They cooked their food over a charcoal fire on top of a tray filled with sand. Or they made a fire in a metal box. They could do this only in a calm sea because the sudden lurching of the ship could tip over the makeshift stove and set the craft afire.

The lower decks were airless and damp, lighted only by a glimmer of candlelight over the ship's compass.

The *Speedwell* and the *Mayflower* had to be made fit for passengers. But the passengers would live on these vessels much as the sailors did.

The *Speedwell* was overhauled. She was scrubbed down and repaired. She was refitted with taller masts and bigger sails, which would enable her to keep up with the *Mayflower*, a larger, stronger ship.

The *Mayflower* was called a "sweet" ship. Her cargo had been wine, which left her timbers with a clean smell. Nevertheless, she too was scrubbed down and her rigging tightened for the ocean crossing.

How Did the Voyage Begin?

IT WAS THE LAST DAY of July 1620 when the Separatists took the first step of their voyage to America. With friends, families, and their pastor, John Robinson, they boarded a barge near their homes at the Rapenburg Canal in Leyden. The barge slowly wound its way into the Vliet Canal and reached Delfshaven eight hours later. There they saw the *Speedwell*, tied to the dock, ready for her passengers.

For their last night in Holland they were sheltered in a building near the Old Church on the canal. Food and drink made it a festive night that rang with laughter and religious songs.

The next morning, August 1, dawned thick with mist rising from the river Maas. It hung like a cloud over the Voorhaven Quay. Crowds had gathered to bid the emigrants farewell. There were friends from Amsterdam and townspeople who had heard of the young people venturing to the New World.

DELFSHAVEN, HOLLAND

Families were separating. They clung to each other, weeping, tears streaming down their faces.

Who traveled on the Speedwell?

The sad, weeping Dorothy Bradford held tight to her little son, John, whom she was leaving in Holland in the care of another family. With her husband, William, she was sailing on the *Speedwell*. Mary Brewster was traveling with her two young sons, Wrestling and Love. Her two daughters, Fear and Patience, remained behind with an older brother, Jonathan. Her husband, William, sought by police for printing illegal literature, was still in hiding. Some men, like Doctor Fuller, traveled alone. Others had their sons with them, while their wives remained behind in Holland with younger children.

A few entire families were making the voyage together. There were the Allertons. Isaac Allerton was a tailor. He, his wife, Mary, and their three children, Bartholomew, Remember, and Mary, were looking forward to the venture. Mrs. Allerton was pregnant. Susanna White was also pregnant. She was making the voyage with her husband and three-year-old son, Resolved. Among her possessions was a cradle for the new baby, whose birth she expected in the New World.

There was Edward Winslow and his wife, Elizabeth. And Mary Cushman and her stepson, Thomas.

In all, there were forty people—slight, bearded men, children, and young women with babies in arms.

Pastor Robinson led a final prayer. The emigrants pulled away from loving embraces and boarded the *Speedwell*. There was last minute frantic waving from shore and ship. In a final salute the *Speedwell* fired off a cannon and a volley of musket fire.

The ship sailed on the broad river Maas into the North Sea. The bright Dutch flag waved from her mast. Cannon stuck out of portholes to protect her from pirates. She moved down the North Sea, through the narrow Strait of Dover into the English Channel. The *Speedwell* was on her way to Southampton, England.

Where Did the Saints and Strangers Meet?

FIVE DAYS AFTER LEAVING Delfshaven, the *Speedwell* slipped into the West Quay of Southampton, England. She dropped anchor next to a ship three times her size. It was the *Mayflower*, which had arrived from London the week before with the London recruits.

The Saints and Strangers met for the first time on the quay of Southampton outside the old fortress wall. They embraced each other with warmth, eager to get along well for the long venture ahead.

The children quickly became friends, running in and out of the boxes and crates lining the dock. They were curious about the large gaping holes in the fortress wall, and they stuck their heads through them. They could see the snug cottages lining the sloping streets of the town.

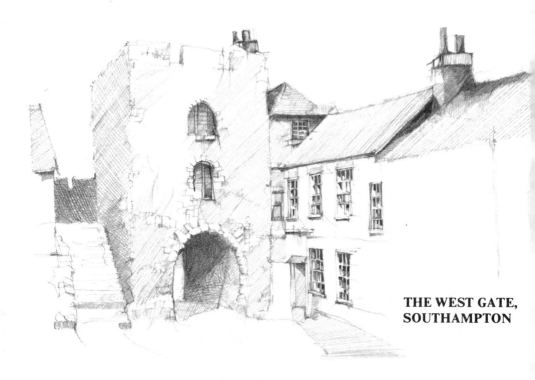

THE WEST GATE, SOUTHAMPTON

How did the Leyden people look?

The Leyden people were at last back in England. For many it was a touching moment, to stand on English soil after an absence of twelve years. They looked odd in their drab, severe clothes. Yet there was something simple and dignified in their appearance as they stood on the busy pier surrounded by the clutter of cargo and lounging sailors.

The men wore steeple hats with broad brims. A silver buckle held in place a ribbon that encircled the crown. Their doublets and breeches were made of tough cloth and they wore heavy leather shoes and woolen stockings.

The women wore simple, dark hooded cloaks that covered them from head to toe. The hoods, tied

[54]

under the chin with a bowknot, gave each face a demure look. Underneath the cloaks were long-sleeved dresses of russet brown or dark green trimmed with plain linen cuffs and a broad fall-away linen collar. The children were dressed like their parents.

The Strangers, on the other hand, made a vivid splash of color. Though poor, they dressed in the bright styles of the day. Lace, buttons, braid, and feathers trimmed their garments.

THE STRANGERS ON THE MAYFLOWER

[55]

Who were some of the Strangers?

Miles Standish and his wife, Rose, were two of the Strangers. Standish was so short the Indians would call him "Captain Shrimp." He had flaming red hair, a red face, and a mean temper. At his side dangled a sword, a reminder that he was a professional soldier who had fought in many wars in Europe.

There was also the shopkeeper William Mullins with his wife and two children, Joseph and Priscilla. And the large Hopkins family, also shopkeepers. Stephen Hopkins had tried to get to America once before, but his ship had been wrecked in the Bermuda Islands. His pregnant wife, Elizabeth, would be good company for the two pregnant women from Leyden. There were also the Billingtons, Tilleys, Chiltons, and many others. In all, about seventy Strangers had been recruited for the voyage.

A strong young man, John Alden, was working in Southampton as a cooper, making casks and tubs. He found the venture unfolding before him so exciting that he signed up for a year with the company. (He stayed on in America and married Priscilla Mullins.)

The Strangers, like the Separatists, were plain, ordinary people with common sense and intelligence. As they stood on the quay at Southampton, each was filled with private dreams. Some dreamed of owning land, others of becoming merchants. Most of them hoped to raise themselves out of the low class in which they had been trapped in England. They wanted to be able to talk up and have a voice in government.

What Delayed the Voyage?

ON THE WAY FROM Delfshaven the *Speedwell* turned out to be a cranky vessel. Skipper Reynolds noticed she was out of balance and leaky. In Southampton he ordered shipwrights to examine her thoroughly. To put her in better sailing trim they shifted her cargo and ballast. And to prevent leakage they recaulked her seams. After a week of repairs they declared the *Speedwell* ready to continue the voyage.

But there were other problems. Thomas Weston, who had arranged for the financing of the project, came down to Southampton from London. He wanted to say goodbye to the emigrants, but he also wanted them to sign a new contract. Two harsh terms had been added to the agreement.

The businessmen now wanted the colonists to work seven days a week for the joint venture. The Separatists insisted on having two days in which to do their own work.

And the businessmen now demanded that the homes of the colonists become the property of the company. The Separatists said that these homes, which they would build for themselves, should remain their private property.

Weston became enraged when the emigrants refused to sign the new agreement. He shouted, "Stand on your own legs!" and he returned to London. Though he and the businessmen were still financially responsible for the project, he refused to provide the small sum of money needed to pay the port dues to clear the ships.

The emigrants had no money. In order to get the voyage on its way they sold off some tubs of butter from their provisions to pay the necessary port fees.

After a discouraging week the *Speedwell* and the *Mayflower* were then free to sail out of Southampton for the New World.

What happened to the Speedwell?

On August 15 the *Speedwell* and the *Mayflower* sailed into the shallow, choppy water of the English Channel.

On the *Speedwell* there was a special celebration. William Brewster had managed to slip past police officials and secretly board the vessel. With their favorite elder among them the Separatists cheerfully settled down in the cramped quarters of the hold of the ship. They could barely stand up straight under the low deck of the ship that was their roof.

The channel weather was stormy. Strong head winds and a rough sea slowed down the progress of the ships. The pounding waves tossed the *Speedwell* about as if she were a puppet on a loose string. She heeled over so far it seemed that she would have real trouble righting herself. And she began to leak! They

**BOARDING THE MAYFLOWER
AT SOUTHAMPTON**

THE MAYFLOWER A

THE SPEEDWELL

could not stop the water that "came in as at a mole hole."

Captain Reynolds signaled the *Mayflower* that the *Speedwell* was in trouble. The two ships set course for Dartmouth, the nearest port.

In Dartmouth expert carpenters spent ten days going over the *Speedwell*. They repaired her leaks, again shifted her cargo for better trim, then pronounced her safe for the voyage.

On September 2 the two ships once again made their way into the English Channel. This time they were lucky. Good weather day after day eased their progress. They cleared the stony cliffs of Land's End, the last bit of England jutting into the sea. The emigrants could look back at the fading shores of their homeland.

The ships sailed on. Passengers prayed there would be no treacherous storms. Even on a calm sea, the vessels rolled and pitched. Many children, grownups, and even crew members groaned with seasickness.

They had logged three hundred miles westward when the *Speedwell* sent out a distress signal. She was leaking again! Skipper Reynolds called the situation dangerous. They would have to put back to England or risk sinking at sea.

The *Mayflower* kept a protective eye on the *Speedwell* as the two ships once more headed back to land. This time they sailed into the deep, snug harbor of Plymouth, England.

The best shipwrights in Plymouth examined every inch of the *Speedwell*. Her condition was something of a mystery. She leaked at sea, although in port she was tight and strong. They could not explain it, but they would not take a chance when the ship faced an Atlantic crossing. They declared that the *Speedwell* should not make the voyage! She would have to be abandoned.

[62]

Who Sailed on the Mayflower?

DECISIONS HAD TO be made quickly. All of August and half of September were gone. The ships would be heading into the season's ocean storms. And the emigrants had hoped to reach America in time to plant crops for an autumn harvest.

The delays had worn down their health. For seven weeks they had been living on damp decks, eating little food because their provisions and fresh water were running dangerously low. Tempers were short. There were arguments and complaints. The crew threatened to walk off the ship because the emigrants, who knew nothing about sailing vessels, were interfering in their work.

How many passengers could the *Mayflower* hold? Who would continue on to America? Who would return to London? Could the *Mayflower* sail alone across the ocean?

Eighteen passengers were considered unfit for the voyage. Among them were families with many children, the sick and the frightened. After sad, tearful goodbyes, they boarded the *Speedwell* for the return to London. In London the businessmen sold the *Speedwell.* Once more she became an ordinary cargo vessel.

There were now 102 passengers on the *Mayflower.* Thirty-five Leyden emigrants had moved over, with their belongings, from the *Speedwell* to join the 67 London recruits. In addition the *Mayflower* carried a crew of 30 and all the cargo.

The *Mayflower* sailed out of Plymouth, England, on September 16, 1620, to begin her voyage to America.

Though the Separatists were in the minority, they dominated the ship. Knit together by strong, common bonds, they were a forceful group. The *Mayflower* rocked with their songs, sermons, and prayers through the many weeks of the voyage.

What Did They Take with Them?

THE CARGO THE EMIGRANTS decided they needed for the voyage was crammed into the hold of the *Mayflower*.

Food

They had on board crates of vegetables, lemons and limes, and boxes of hardtack (dried biscuits). There were sacks of flour, potatoes, dried beans, and peas; tubs of butter; slabs of bacon; jars of oil; and bags of salt. There were hogsheads of beer and brandy, barrels of salted-down pork and beef, and casks of fresh water.

They also took along seeds for planting their first crops on the new land.

Furnishings

Families brought small chests packed with personal belongings, blankets, linens, and clothes. Some

also brought small pieces of furniture, like the cradle Mrs. White carried with her from Leyden. It came in handy when she gave birth on November 20 in the cabin of the *Mayflower*.

They took along dishes, kettles, pots, pans, needles, and thread.

For trading with the Indians there were trinkets such as glass beads, small mirrors, cotton fabric, and bits and pieces of junk. An iron pot was later traded for many fur skins.

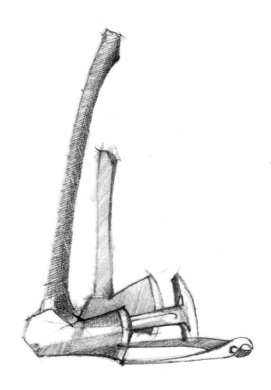

Tools

The hold of the ship was crowded with axes for cutting down trees, hoes for digging, and scythes for clearing the fields. There were tools for the artisans— the smith, the roper, the cobbler, the tailor, and the carpenter; and there were nets for fishing.

Guns and Armor

The ship carried standard military equipment of the time. It included helmets, steel breast-and-back plates, swords, cutlasses, pikes, and muskets. There was more than enough to defend the colony against the Indians, who used only bows and arrows.

Books

The emigrants carried their Bibles and other religious books with them. Doctor Fuller took along his medical books.

Music

The Separatists considered musical instruments frivolous. They sang their psalms without musical accompaniment. The *Book of Psalmes*, or psalter, they

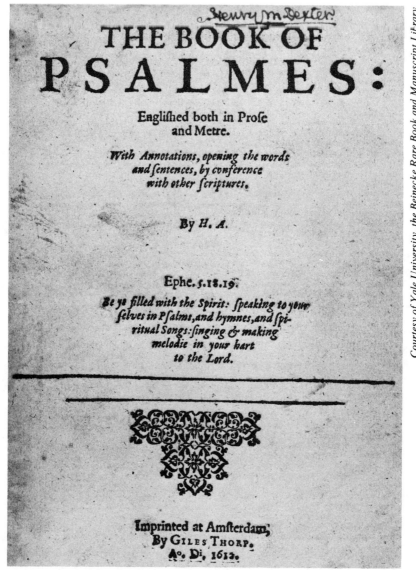

THE PSALM-BOOK OF HENRY AINSWORTH

brought with them was prepared by Henry Ainsworth, a biblical scholar and dissenter who had fled
to Amsterdam from England.

The woodlands near Plymouth Colony echoed to

Pſalm. C.   353

a Preiſt, oʒ Sacrificer, is the name of the Kings cheif officer, as in 2. Sam. 8, 18. Davids ſonns
were Cohéns, (Cheif-rulers, Aularchai as the Greek termeth them;) which is expounded in
1.Chron. 18. 17. to be the firſt (oʒ Cheif) at the Kings hand. It hath the name of miniſtration,
Iſa.61,6,10. and was a title ſpeciallp given to Aaron and his ſonns, that miniſtred unto God
in the Sanctuarie. Exo.28.3.4.41.   caled] aʒ were caling: that is, pʒaped foʒ the people, as
Exod.32, 11. &c. Num.14,17,19.& 16.22,46. 1.Sam.7.9. & 12.19.23. Hereupon Moſes & Samuel were noted foʒ cheif interceſſoʒs with God , Ier. 15,1.   ʋ. 7. of a clowd] as Exo.
33.9. Num.16,42. and this noteth Gods favour, but with ſome obſcuritp: and ſo is inferiour
to the mediation of Chʒiſt, who hath without clowds oʒ ſhadowes obtepnd eternal re-
demption foʒ us; that we map goe boldlp to the thʒone of grace, foʒ to receiu mercy and find
grace to help in time of need. Heb. 4,14,16. & 7,25. & 9.11,12.   ʋ. 8. a God forgiving]
a mighty-God that pardonedſt, oʒ tookeſt away , to weet, the puniſſment of their ſpn: ſee Pſ.
25,18.   and taking] oʒ though thou tookeſt vengeance.   on their practiſes] theirs
that is the peoples, foʒ whom Moſes pʒaped , as Num. 14, 20, 21, 23. Exod. 32, 14,34,35. oʒ
theirs ; that is, Moſes and Aarons ſynns; which God puniſhed and would not be intreated;
as Num. 20,12. Deut. 3,23,24,25,26.

Pſalm. 100.

1.   A pſalm for confeſſion:
SHowt ye-triumphantly to Iehovah, al
the earth.

2. Serv ye Iehovah with gladnes: come
before him, with ſinging-joy.

3. Know ye, that Iehovah he is God:
he made us, and not we: his people, &
ſheep of his paſture.

4. Enter ye his gates, with confeſſion; his courts with praiſe: confeſs ye to
him, bleſs ye his name.

5. For Iehovah is good, his mercy is
for ever: & his faith, unto generation
& generation.

Pſalm. 100.

1. SHowt to Iehovah, al the earth. 2. Serv ye
Iehovah with gladnes: before him come with ſing-
ing-merth. 3. Know, that Iehovah he God is:
Its he that made us, and not Wee;
his folk, and ſheep of his feeding.
4. O with confeſſion enter yee
his gates, his courtyards with praiſing:
confeſs to him, bleſs ye his name.
5. Becauſe Iehovah he good is:
his mercy ever, is the ſame:
and his faith, unto al ages.

Annotations.

Verſ. 1. for confeſſion] for the publick praiſe of God, with thanks for his mercies.
ʋ. 2. ſinging] oʒ thrilling , ſhowting-merth.   ʋ.3. made us] this woʒd is uſed both
foʒ our firſt treation in nature, Gen. 1, 26. and foʒ the making of us lpe and eʒcellent with
graces and bleſſings, as 1.Sam.12,6. Deut.32,6. Iſa.43,7.& 29.23. Ephe.2,10.   and not we]
oʒ,and his we are: as the Hebʒue in the margine readeth it. Both ſenſes are good.
ſheep] oʒ flock which he feedeth. See Ezek.34,30,31. Pſal.95.7.   ʋ. 4. confeſſion] the
ſacrifice of thanks was thus named; 2. Chron.29,31. Ier.17.26.   ʋ. 5. faith] oʒ, faith-
fulnes: truth, in perfoʒming his pʒomiſes.

Ii 3   Pſalm. CI.

THE ONE-HUNDREDTH PSALM

these religious songs for more than seventy years.

The poet Henry Longfellow, in "The Courtship of Miles Standish," mentions that John Alden finds Priscilla singing the One-hundredth Psalm.

> Open wide on her lap lay the well-worn
> psalm-book of Ainsworth,
> Printed in Amsterdam, the words and the
> music together.

Servants

Poor as most of the families were, there were nevertheless twelve servants and six orphan children among them. They would become known as indentured servants and would do the difficult work of building the colony. They were under contract for seven years, during which time they had no freedom. They could not marry without permission of their masters, and they could be sold from one family to another. In return for their bondage they were given passage, shelter, food, and clothing. At the end of their term they regained their freedom and were granted some acres of land.

What Kind
of Crossing
Did They Have?

FOR A MONTH THE *Mayflower* sailed peacefully on. At night the light of an oil lamp flickered on deck. Below, a candle lantern threw its weak light over the compass.

Then in mid-ocean storms broke. The raging sea crashed against the ship. Roaring winds battered her night and day and forced open her deck seams. Water poured through them down on the sick and frightened passengers below. John Howland, a servant with the Carver family, came up on deck for a bit of fresh air and was immediately swept overboard. He grabbed hold of a rope trailing behind the ship and was pulled back to safety by a sailor with a boathook.

As the storm's fury increased, one of the main beams cracked. No one knew what to do. There were hours of turmoil with talk of turning back to England. But level heads prevailed. The ship was carefully gone over from stem to stern and found to be basically sound. The crew repaired the damaged beam and caulked her seams.

The pregnant women in particular suffered from the long weeks and months of the voyage. The rolling, pitching ship made them seasick and weak. Two of them gave birth on the *Mayflower*. Elizabeth Hopkins's baby boy was born in mid-ocean. They named him Oceanus. While the ship was anchored off New England, Susanna White gave birth to a son they called Peregrine, which means wanderer. On land during the first freezing winter, Mary Allerton had a still-born child. She herself died a few days later.

Dorothy Bradford never set foot on the soil of America. She was a frail young woman, perhaps grieving for her little son in Holland. While the *Mayflower* was anchored off land, she fell or jumped off the ship.

The children amused themselves with games they made up. The older boys wished they could join the crew, who worked barefoot on the deck. They marveled when the sailors climbed up and down the rigging like skilled acrobats.

A couple of youngsters were troublemakers. Francis Billington, eight years old, almost blew up the *Mayflower* when he shot off a musket near a keg of gunpowder.

On the sixty-sixth day of the voyage from Plymouth, England, the Pilgrims sighted land.

Why Are the Pilgrims Important?

THE PILGRIMS LAID THE foundation for some of our basic ideas.

In many ways this country began on the rocky coast where the Pilgrims landed. The small band of men, women, and children clung to a stony strip of land and built the first permanent colony in New England.

They were a stubborn people, determined to set down roots in the rocky soil. During the first cold winter, starvation, poor housing, and disease killed off half the band. Only with the help of the Indians did the others survive. They had no time to weep. And they did not complain. In the warmth of the first spring they turned over the soil and put in seeds. The Indians taught them how to plant corn. In the fall of 1621 they gathered their first harvest.

They, and those who joined them in later years, brought ideas and habits from the Old World. But they had to change to survive in the wilderness. They had been farmers, artisans, workers. They became fishermen, lumbermen, and fur traders. They remained deeply religious, hardworking, and frugal. But they also became inventive, and shrewd, bold businessmen. Above all they were fiercely independent.

They pushed their way north and west into new land. Wherever they went they left their mark by setting up laws for self-government.

Their first laws were embodied in the Mayflower Compact, an agreement signed by forty-one men on board ship. At that time they chose their first governor, John Carver.

Not everyone was equal in the new communities, but it was far better than the feudal systems of Europe.

Indian life and culture came to an end wherever the Pilgrims settled. Though the Indians taught them how to live in the woodlands, the Pilgrims never overcame their idea that the Indians were savage and inferior. The land that had belonged to the Indians was settled by English-speaking people with ties to England.

In the struggles to build a new life the Separatists and the London recruits drew closer together. And history treated them as one. For years they were referred to as the ancestors or the forefathers. Sometimes they were called newcomers or first settlers.

More than 170 years later, in the 1790s, a speaker at a celebration of "Forefathers Day" referred to them as the Pilgrims and the Pilgrim Fathers. These terms became popular, especially "Pilgrim Fathers."

Today, when it is recognized that women and children worked equally hard as the men to build the new colony, we call them the Pilgrims.

Places to Visit

YOU CAN FOLLOW THE Pilgrim trail on a map and trace the lives of the Pilgrims from their birthplaces in England to Holland and to America. Or, if you travel in these countries, you will find plaques, monuments, and memorials that mark Pilgrim sites.

Here are some Pilgrim places:

Scrooby

In Scrooby, England, a plaque marks St. Wilfred's Church, where William Brewster was baptized and where he attended services with his family until he became a Separatist. There is also a plaque that marks the site of "THE ANCIENT MANOR HOUSE WHERE LIVED WILLIAM BREWSTER FROM 1588 TO 1608 . . ."

A little to the northeast of Scrooby, in Austerfield, the register in St. Helen's Church records the birth of

William Bradford. And southeast of Scrooby John Robinson's birthplace is marked in Sturton le Steeple.

Boston, England

You follow the trail in England east to the seaport of Boston. An imposing memorial with an inset tablet will remind you that the Pilgrims "SET SAIL [from Boston] ON THEIR FIRST ATTEMPT TO FIND RELIGIOUS FREEDOM ACROSS THE SEAS." In the Boston Guildhall there are prison cells. A tablet inserted in the wall above them says that the Pilgrims were imprisoned in those cells when they were caught trying to flee from England.

MEMORIAL IN BOSTON, ENGLAND

Leyden

Leyden is alive with reminders of the Pilgrims. In the old quarter quiet canals still flow. Tiled roofs of gabled houses shine through the wide-spreading branches of old trees. And students still argue important issues at the university. The library is rich with research material on the Pilgrims. There are books, photos, maps, and articles.

It is easy to locate the hulking stone structure of St. Peter's Church. On one of its walls is a bronze tablet "IN MEMORY OF JOHN ROBINSON ..." The Green Gate, where the Pilgrims worshiped for eleven years, is now an almshouse. Around the small garden are neat little cottages that once housed the poor Separatists. Only a memorial plaque on the front of the building reminds you that "ON THIS SPOT LIVED, TAUGHT AND DIED, JOHN ROBINSON, 1611-1625."

Along the narrow, damp streets you will find Choir Alley, which was the side entrance to the Brewster house on Stink Alley. Up the stairway in the attic Brewster turned out the seditious pamphlets on what is now called the Pilgrim Press.

If you stand on Nuns Bridge, you can watch the Rapenburg Canal flow by. It enters the Vliet and then flows on to Delfshaven, where the Separatists boarded the *Speedwell.*

Delfshaven

In Delfshaven the old quarter along the Voorhaven Quay is being restored. You enter the Old Church, now called the Pilgrim Fathers Church. It is filled with memorial tablets, paintings, and stained glass insets depicting the departure of the Pilgrims on the *Speedwell.*

You can take a short walk to the end of Voorhaven Quay, where the canal flows into the river Maas.

[77]

There, another plaque in English and Dutch advises you that "THIS IS THE STARTING POINT OF THE 'SPEEDWELL.' " As you look out on the Maas, you may imagine seeing children, women, and men leaning far out over the railing of the frail sailing vessel, waving frantic goodbyes to families and friends, most of whom they would never again see.

Southampton

The *Speedwell* sailed down the North Sea to Southampton, where it met the *Mayflower*. A plaque on the West Gate of the ancient wall reminds you of the Pilgrim stopover. More imposing is the tall memorial shaft outside the old wall, which tells you "BOTH SHIPS SAILED [from Southampton] ON AUGUST 15, 1620, FOR THE NEW WORLD."

Plymouth, England

Plymouth, England, is busy with Pilgrim reminders. That port celebrates its historic role of having been the point from which the *Mayflower* finally sailed to America. You go down to the Barbican, at the ancient quay. There you see Island House, where it is said a few Pilgrims spent the night and refreshed themselves when the ships were in port. On the west pier you will see the *Mayflower* Memorial. In front of it, a stone set in the pavement reads "MAYFLOWER, 1620." The plaque will tell you, "THE PILGRIM FATHERS SAILED FROM PLYMOUTH IN THE 'MAYFLOWER' . . . TO SETTLE IN NEW PLYMOUTH AND TO LAY THE FOUNDATION OF THE NEW ENGLAND STATES."

Plymouth, Massachusetts

Plymouth, Massachusetts, is Pilgrim land of the United States. Each year thousands of people, especially schoolchildren, visit there to enjoy Pilgrim history. On every side there are landmarks. *Mayflower*

[78]

MONUMENT IN PLYMOUTH, ENGLAND

II, a replica of the original *Mayflower*, stands in port. You can board the ship and walk on its decks, examine its rigging, and learn how the ship made its voyage. You will find Plymouth Rock at the waterfront housed in an ornate Grecian structure. A carved sarcophagus lists the Pilgrims who died the first year. There is Plimoth Plantation, a reconstruction of the colony as it was in the 1620s. There you can visualize life at that time. There are monuments, statues, paintings, museums, and many other reminders of the small band that planted a colony on these shores.

Suggested Further Reading

American Heritage Society. *The Pilgrims and Plymouth Colony.* New York: American Heritage Publishing Co., 1961.

Coblentz, Catherine. *The Bells of Leyden Sing.* New York: Longmans, Green & Co., 1944. Fiction.

Daringer, Helen F. *Debbie of the Green Gate.* New York: Harcourt, Brace & Co., 1950. Fiction.

Foster, Genevieve. *The World of Captain John Smith.* New York: Charles Scribner's & Sons, 1959.

Fox, Levi. *Shakespeare's England, A Pictorial Source Book.* New York: G. P. Putnam's Sons, 1972.

Greenleaf, Margery. *Dirk, A Story of the Struggle for Freedom in Holland, 1572-1574.* Chicago: Follett Publishing Co., 1971. Fiction.

Hall, Elvajean. *Pilgrim Stories*, revised and expanded, from *Pilgrim Stories*, by Margaret Pumphrey. New York: Rand McNally & Co., 1961. Fiction.

Hall-Quest, Olga W. *How the Pilgrims Came to Plymouth*. New York: E. P. Dutton & Co., 1946.

Longfellow, Henry Wadsworth. "The Courtship of Miles Standish" in *Favorite Poems of Henry Wadsworth Longfellow,* edited by H. S. Canby. New York: Doubleday & Co., 1967.

Morison, Samuel Eliot. *The Story of the "Old Colony" of New Plymouth*. New York: Alfred A. Knopf, 1963.

Smith, Brooks E., and Meredith, Robert, eds. *Pilgrim Courage*. Boston: Little Brown & Co., 1962. From a firsthand account by William Bradford, selected episodes from his original history, *Of Plimoth Plantation*.

Taylor, Duncan. *The Elizabethan Age*. New York: Roy Publishers, 1954.

38567